Benjamin and the Box

Story and pictures by

ALAN BAKER

J. B. Lippincott Company • Philadelphia and New York

U.S. Library of Congress Cataloging in Publication Data
Baker, Alan.   Benjamin and the box.
SUMMARY: Benjamin Hamster is curious about the contents of a box he cannot open.
[1. Hamsters—Fiction.   2. Boxes—Fiction] I. Title.
PZ7.B1688Be   [E]   77-23870   ISBN-0-397-31774-3

Hmm, what's this?

A box!
I wonder how you open it?

Soon find out.
One twist of the screwdriver and . . .

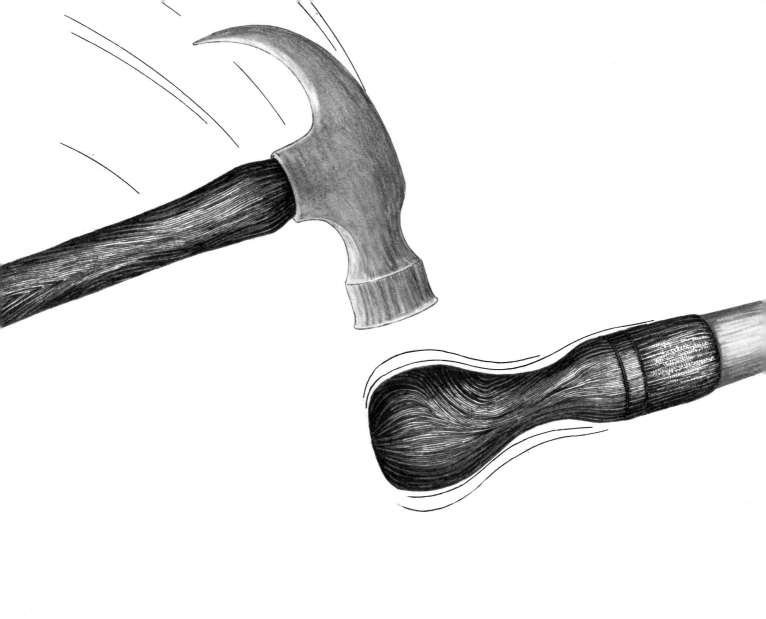

Oh well, this hammer should
do the trick.

Not quite.
Push the screwdriver
in a bit further.

That's better.
Now the hammer again . . .
Bang! Bang!

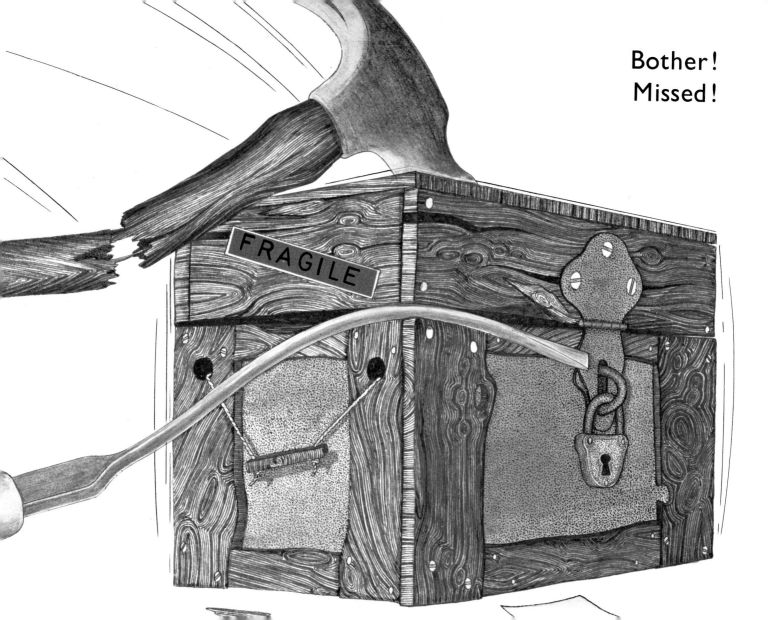

. . . Let's try something
a little more subtle.

Hey Presto!
Benjamin Hamster springs
into action.

Abracadabra!

Open box!

Hmm, I never did believe in magic.

What's this? A padlock.
How silly of me not to have
seen that before.

Soon have this off.

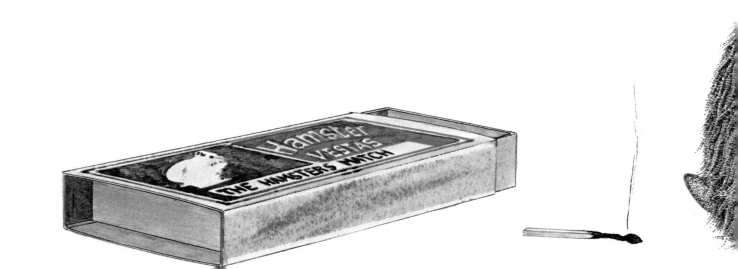

Oh dear, I've set the box alight.

Water, quick!

Whoooosh!

Time for brute force.

Hey! What's going on?

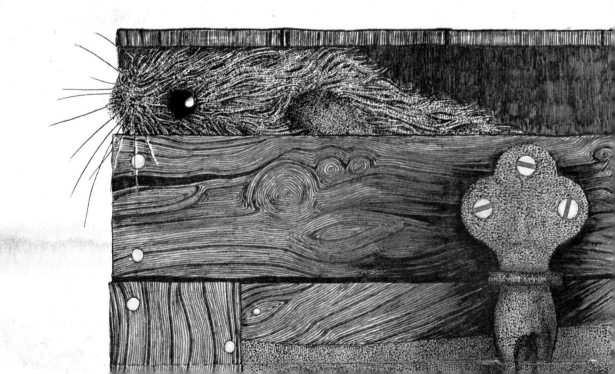